A New True Book

THE CONSTITUTION

By Warren Colman

CHILDREN'S PRESS
A Division of Grolier Publishing
Sherman Turnpike
Danbury, Connecticut 06816

Pickets demonstrate in favor of the
Equal Rights Amendment.

PHOTO CREDITS

AP/Wide World Photos, Inc.—31, 42 (left)

© Cameramann International, Ltd.—4 (top), 6
(left), 29 (left)

Nawrocki Stock Photo:
© Jeff Apoian—21 (left)
© Wm. S. Nawrocki—13 (3 photos)
© Jim Wright—6 (right)

Photo Source International/© Three Lions—7,
23

Marilyn Gartman Agency:
© Lee Balterman—4 (bottom left)
© Herwig—41 (right)
© Photri—2, 29 (right)

The Granger Collection—28 (right)

Historical Pictures Service, Chicago—8
(2 photos), 9, 14 (2 photos), 15 (left and
center), 17, 18, 36, 37

Journalism Services:
© Joseph Jacobson—6 (middle)
© Paul Gero—26 (left)

© H. Armstrong Roberts/© Camerique—39
(2 photos)

Roloc Color Slides—Cover, 4 (bottom right), 11,
15 (right), 21 (right), 22, 26 (left), 28 (left), 38,
41 (left), 42 (right), 45

Tom Stack & Associates: © Brian Parker—34
(left)

© National Geographic Society/Supreme Court
Historical Society—32

Art: © Horizon Graphics—25, 27, 34

Cover: The signing of the Constitution

Library of Congress Cataloging-in-Publication Data

Colman, Warren.
    The Constitution.

    (A New true book)
    Includes index.
    Summary: Describes, in simple terms, how the
Constitution was conceived, written, and ratified in
1788, explaining the document's basic concepts and Bill
of Rights.
    1.   United States—Constitutional law—Juvenile
literature. [1.   United States—Constitutional law]
I.   Title.
KF4550.Z9C58   1987   342.73′029   86-30968
ISBN 0-516-01231-2   347.30229

Childrens Press, Chicago
Copyright ©1987 by Regensteiner Publishing Enterprises, Inc.
All rights reserved. Published simultaneously in Canada.
Printed in the United States of America.
        7 8 9 10 R 96 95

TABLE OF CONTENTS

Baseball could not be played without rules.

OUR COUNTRY'S MAIN RULE

Think what a baseball game would be like without rules. How many innings would there be? How many strikes would it take before the batter is out? Without rules, nobody would know how to play baseball.

Rules tell us what to do. Cities have rules, too. They are often called laws.

Signs tell us what
the traffic laws are.

States have laws. And so
does our country.

The United States of
America has more than two
hundred million people.
With so many people,
there must be thousands
of laws. But there is just
one main law in the
United States. It is called
the Constitution.

The Constitution of the
United States of America

Every other law in the
United States must agree
with it.

The Constitution does
something else, too. It tells
how our government in
Washington, D.C., will be run.

BEFORE THE CONSTITUTION

Once the thirteen colonies in America were ruled by the king of England and his parliament. But by 1765 many colonists did

The colonists protest against British laws such as the Stamp Act (below right) which placed a tax stamp on all newspapers and legal documents. These protests were often stopped by British soldiers (below left).

Trumbull's painting shows the delegates signing the Declaration of Independence. The declaration said, "these United Colonies are, and of right ought to be, free and independent states."

not like the way England ruled them. They said the laws made in England were unfair.

So on July 4, 1776, the leaders in America issued the Declaration of Independence.

The colonists fought the king and his government. And they won.

When the Americans became free, a new set of rules was needed. The new rules would replace the laws of England.

Many American leaders gathered to write the rules. Most of them felt that each state should be like a little country.

The new rules were written. These rules were

The Articles of Confederation was the law of the United States from 1781 to 1789.

called the Articles of
Confederation. Each state
agreed to be friends with
all the other states.

All the states agreed to
work with the government.
But the states would not

let the central government have too much power.

This central government could not raise money with taxes. It could not make agreements with other countries. It could not print money. Each state would have those jobs.

At first people liked the new rules. But as time passed, problems came about. The central government needed an army. But the rules didn't allow it.

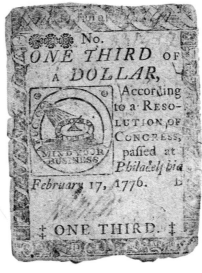

During and after the Revolutionary War the states printed their own paper money. Here are some samples from New Jersey (left) and Pennsylvania (middle and right).

Then the states began to argue. They couldn't agree on borders. Some states would not take money that was printed in other states.

Things just weren't going well. The rules weren't working. So a meeting was called to see if the rules could be changed.

George Washington
(right)
James Madison
(far right)

THE MEETING
IN PHILADELPHIA

The meeting to change
the rules took place in
Philadelphia. All the states,
except Rhode Island, sent
delegates.

George Washington
reached Philadelphia on
May 14, 1787. James
Madison of Virginia,

Alexander Hamilton

Benjamin Franklin

Robert Morris

Alexander Hamilton from
New York, Robert Morris
and Benjamin Franklin
from Pennsylvania were
already there.

The delegates met in
Independence Hall. The
first thing they did was to
elect George Washington
president of the meeting.
Everyone trusted him.

15

Then they tried to decide what to do. Should they change the Articles of Confederation? Or should they throw out the old rules and start over?

The talk went on and on. It was very hot that summer. But to keep the meeting secret the delegates kept the windows shut. They put guards at the doors. To cut down on noise straw was put on the street around Independence Hall.

Independence Hall

That way the delegates
would not hear the
wagons that clattered over
the cobblestones outside.

The meeting room was
hot. But day after day the
delegates argued.

17

Painting of the constitutional convention showing George Washington presiding over delegates.

James Madison and Alexander Hamilton wanted to throw out the old rules. They wanted to make the central government stronger than the state governments. James Madison even had a written plan for this new government in his pocket.

Many delegates said no. They said Madison's rules would make the new government too powerful.

Soon, two groups formed. One side said America would be weak and poor without a strong government. The other side wanted to keep the states as strong as they were.

The two groups talked and talked and talked.

In July there was another problem. The small

states were afraid the new rules would make the big states too strong.

Some delegates wondered if the new government should be ruled by a king. But no one really wanted that. Then what kind of leader should there be?

Slowly these problems were worked out. Once the big problems were taken care of, the small ones were quickly solved.

People may go to Independence Hall (left) and visit the meeting room (above) where the colonists signed the Constitution of the United States.

Each side gave in a little. Each side compromised. Finally by September, everything was decided. The delegates were ready to write the new plan of government.

21

WHAT THE CONSTITUTION SAID

Gouverneur Morris

A small group was elected to write the new set of rules. It was to be called the Constitution of the United States.

James Madison and Alexander Hamilton were elected to the group. Their plan for a stronger central government had won. Gouverneur Morris of New York drafted the Constitution

To many Americans our country's most famous words are "We the People." The final version of the constitution was written by Jacob Shallus, a clerk. He received less than thirty dollars for his work.

by hand. Its opening statement explains why the new rules were written. It is called the Preamble.

We the People of the United States, in order to form a more perfect Union, establish justice, insure domestic tranquility, provide for the common defense, promote the general welfare, and secure the blessing of liberty to ourselves and our posterity, do ordain and establish this Constitution for the United States of America.

The Constitution says
that the central
government should have
three branches. Each
branch has its own job.
No other branch can do
that job.

One branch—the
legislative—makes the laws.

Another branch—the
executive—makes certain
the laws are obeyed.

The third branch—the
judicial—tells what the law
means.

The Constitution gives

THREE BRANCHES OF GOVERNMENT

EXECUTIVE
Law Enforcing

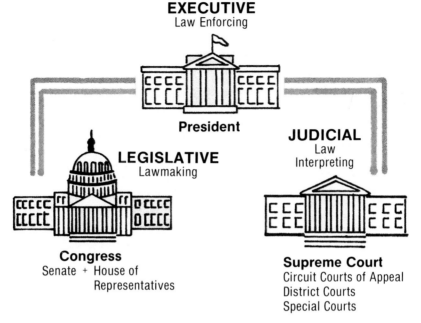

President

LEGISLATIVE
Lawmaking

Congress
Senate + House of
Representatives

JUDICIAL
Law
Interpreting

Supreme Court
Circuit Courts of Appeal
District Courts
Special Courts

the rules for each branch.

The lawmaking branch
must have two parts. One
part is the Senate. Two
lawmakers from each state
serve in the Senate.

The other part is the
House of Representatives.

House of Representatives (above)
and the Senate (right)

Every state has at least
one representative. Big
states have more.

Together the House and
the Senate are called
Congress.

Congress was divided
into two parts to settle the
argument between the states.

UTAH

NEW YORK

U.S. House of Representatives			
one representative per 465,000 Americans.			
Census year	Total	Census year	Total
1787	65	1880	332
1790	106	1890	357
1800	142	1900	391
1810	186	1910	435
1820	213	1930	435
1830	242	1940	435
1840	232	1950	437
1850	237	1960	435
1860	243	1970	435
1870	293	1980	435

The number of representatives each state has is determined by the population of that state.

The small states wanted each state to have the same number of votes in Congress. That would keep the big states from becoming too powerful.

The big states said that was unfair. They said states with more people should have more votes.

The big states and small states finally decided to

27

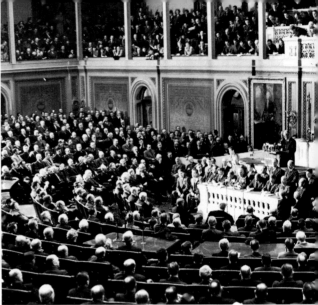

Both President John F. Kennedy (left) and President Franklin
Delano Roosevelt addressed the Congress during their term in office.

compromise. The Senate is
what the small states
wanted. The House of
Representatives is what
the big states wanted.

No law can be passed
by Congress unless both
groups agree to it.

The next part of the

Visitors watch the annual egg rolling contest held on the grounds of the White House, the president's home. Most presidents have worked in the Oval Office (above).

Constitution gives rules for the executive branch.

The Constitution says that the president must be the leader of the executive branch. It says there must be a vice president.

The Constitution tells how the president and

vice president must be elected. Each would serve four-year terms. It tells their duties.

The president was to make sure the laws passed by Congress were obeyed. The president could also make agreements, called treaties, with other governments. He or she could ask people to work in the government. The president could do all these things, but only if Congress agreed.

Lawmakers watch President Ronald Reagan sign a law. From left to right the lawmakers are: Representative Rodino, New Jersey; Senator Simpson, Wyoming; Vice President Bush, and Senator Thurmond, South Carolina. Since 1789 U.S. presidents have vetoed more than 2000 bills.

This rule made sure that the Congress approved what the president did.

The president must sign the laws passed by Congress. If there is a law the president does not like it will not be signed. This is called a veto.

Nine justices sit on the Supreme Court. From left to right in the first row are: Associate Justices Sandra Day O'Connor and Harry A. Blackmun, Chief Justice William H. Rehnquist, Associate Justices John P. Stevens and Antonin Scalia. Associate Justices Clarence Thomas, Anthony Kennedy, David H. Souter, and Ruth Bader Ginsburg are standing in the second row.

The next part of the Constitution gives rules for the judicial branch.

The Constitution says this branch should be made up of courts and judges. It says the president chooses the judges. But the Senate must agree with the president's choices. It says judges can have their jobs for life. But if a judge breaks the law, he or she might be removed from office by the Congress.

The delegates at Philadelphia did not want any branch of government to be the most powerful. They wanted each branch to have some power over the other branches.

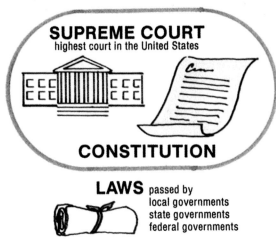

The Supreme Court building
in Washington, D.C.

The rest of the
Constitution allows states
to make their own laws.
But it says the laws in the
Constitution are the most
important laws.

It also tells how changes
may be made to the

Constitution. The changes were to be called amendments.

The last part tells how the Constitution could become the law of the United States. Nine states would have to vote for it.

The delegates talked and argued about the Constitution. But finally, on September 17, 1787, thirty-nine of the fifty-five delegates in Philadelphia signed the Constitution.

Delegates sign the Constitution at the Constitutional Convention

The delegates' work was done. Now they had to go back to their states and fight for the new rules and the new government.

TWENTY-SIX AMENDMENTS

Delaware was the first state to approve the Constitution. New Hampshire was the ninth state to sign in 1788.

Still not everyone liked the Constitution. Many

Cartoons attacked the Antifederalists, those people who did not want their states to accept the Constitution.

Patrick Henry
was against
the Constitution.

people thought it did not
say enough about the
rights of the people.
Patrick Henry, said it gave
much too much power
to the central government.

Again, two groups formed.
Finally a compromise
was reached. Everyone
agreed that a list of
freedoms would be
added to the Constitution.

In 1791, ten amendments were added. They are called the Bill of Rights.

The first amendment lists five important freedoms.

• All Americans may worship as they wish.

Freedom of religion is the right of all Americans.

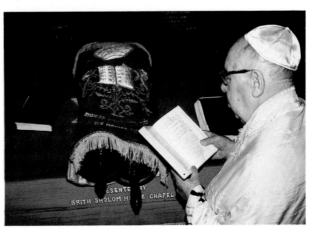

• All Americans may
write about whatever they
want.

• All Americans may
speak about whatever they
want.

• All Americans may
gather together "peaceably."

• All Americans may tell
their governments how
they want things changed.

The other amendments
in the Bill of Rights
protect Americans against
unfair arrests and unfair

Freedom to assemble and to demonstrate against government policy is guaranteed by the First Amendment.

trials. They protect Americans against cruel punishments. They protect American homes and families.

Since 1791 sixteen more amendments have been

Amendments had to be made to the Constitution before women (left) and blacks (right) were given the right to vote.

passed. One of them freed the slaves in 1865. Others allowed blacks and women to vote. The last amendment was passed in 1971. It gave 18-year-olds the right to vote.

A CONSTITUTION FOR ALL TIMES

A lot has happened since the Constitution was written. Once only thirteen states were part of the United States of America. Now there are fifty states in the union.

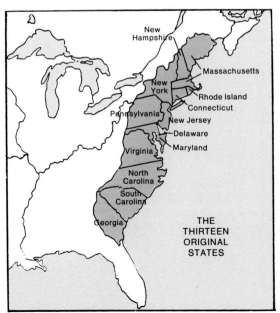

THE THIRTEEN ORIGINAL STATES

New Hampshire
Massachusetts
New York
Rhode Island
Connecticut
Pennsylvania
New Jersey
Delaware
Maryland
Virginia
North Carolina
South Carolina
Georgia

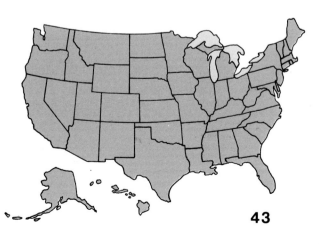

In 1789 most Americans lived on farms or in small towns. Today most live in cities. In the last two hundred years almost everything about the way people live in America has changed dramatically.

But our Constitution has stayed about the same. It has worked well in times of peace. It has worked well in times of war.

We owe a lot to the people who wrote our

East side of the Capitol. The House of Representatives
and the Senate meet in this building.

Constitution. Those wise
men wrote a law that
made America strong. The
Constitution worked then
and it is still working
today.

WORDS YOU SHOULD KNOW

agreement(ah • GREE • mint) — an arrangement, as a contract, in which two or more sides have the same opinion or intention

amendments(ah • MEND • mints) — statements with changes, corrections, or improvements upon the original document

article(AR • tik • il) — one item of a group of statements, as in an agreement, treaty, or contract

Articles of Confederation(AR • tik • ilz UV kun • fed • er • RAY • shun) — the first Constitution adopted in 1781 by the 13 original states, in force till 1788

Bill of Rights(BILL UV RITES) — the first ten amendments to the U.S. Constitution

border(BOR • der) — the line separating one territory from another

central(SEN • tril) — main, chief; the controlling, important part

colonies(KAHL • uh • neez) — regions where people from a distant country settle, but continue to be ruled by the original country

compromise(KOM • pruh • myze) — an arrangement of settling differences in which each agrees to give up some of its demands

confederation(kun • fed • er • RAY • shun) — the union of persons or groups who are in agreement in a common purpose

Congress(KAHNG • ress) — the combined Senate and House of Representatives

declaration(dek • lair • RAY • shun) — a statement; an announcement

delegates(DEL • ih • gits) — persons sent to represent and act for others

elected(ih • LEK • tid) — chosen, picked out, voted for

groups(GROOPS) — a number of persons or things that together relate to a subject or matter in some way

House of Representatives(HOUSE UV rep • pri • ZEN • ta • tivz) — persons elected in each state who represent the people in their wants and directions

independent(in • dih • PEN • dint) — not dependent; free from the control of others

king(KING) — a male ruler of a country whose reign is handed down to his descendants

law(LAW) — rules by which people or organizations are governed

parliament(PAR • lih • mint) — in Great Britain, a body of law-makers, representing the people

preamble(PRE • am • bil) — the opening sentences of an important document explaining the reasons for what follows

Senate(SEN • it) — the group of elected persons, two from each state, who are the highest body of law-makers in the nation

senator(SEN • ih • ter) — an elected member of the Senate; holds office for six years

state(STAYT) — one territory in which its people adopt their own laws, and, joined with other such territories, forms a nation, as the United States

taxes(TAX • iz) — amounts required by government from its members for its support

veto(VEE • toh) — disapprove, prevent from becoming law

INDEX

About the author

Warren Colman is a writer-director-producer. He is president of a company that makes educational filmstrips and videos, as well as training and promotional media for businesses. He has a bachelor's and a master's degree from Northwestern University.

DATE DUE